Travel America's
Exploring Ellis Island

by Emma Huddleston

FOCUS
READERS

BEACON

www.focusreaders.com

Focus Readers is distributed by North Star Editions:
sales@northstareditions.com | 888-417-0195

Produced for Focus Readers by Red Line Editorial.

Photographs ©: Felix Mizioznikov/Shutterstock Images, cover, 1; Everett Historical/ Shutterstock Images, 4, 7, 8, 11, 13, 19, 20; Matej Hudovernik/Shutterstock Images, 14–15, 29; monkeybusinessimages/iStockphoto, 16; felixmizioznikov/iStockphoto, 22; Red Line Editorial, 25; Dave Cantor/AP Images, 27

Library of Congress Cataloging-in-Publication Data
Names: Huddleston, Emma, author.
Title: Exploring Ellis Island / by Emma Huddleston.
Description: Lake Elmo, MN : Focus Readers, 2020. | Series: Travel
    America's landmarks | Audience: Grade 4 to 6. | Includes bibliographical
    references and index.
Identifiers: LCCN 2018060039 (print) | LCCN 2019000530 (ebook) | ISBN
    9781641859844 (pdf) | ISBN 9781641859202 (hosted ebook) | ISBN
    9781641857826 (hardcover) | ISBN 9781641858519 (paperback)
Subjects: LCSH: Ellis Island Immigration Station (N.Y. and N.J.)--Juvenile
    literature. | Ellis Island (N.J. and N.Y.)--History--Juvenile literature. |
    United States--Emigration and immigration--History--Juvenile literature.
Classification: LCC JV6484 (ebook) | LCC JV6484 .H84 2020 (print) | DDC
    974.9/27--dc23
LC record available at https://lccn.loc.gov/2018060039

Printed in the United States of America
Mankato, MN
May, 2019

About the Author

Emma Huddleston lives in the Twin Cities with her husband. She enjoys writing children's books, but she likes reading novels even more. When she is not writing or reading, she likes to stay active by running and swing dancing. She thinks America's landmarks are fascinating and wants to visit them all.

Table of Contents

Chapter 1

Immigration Station

In the early 1900s, thousands of **immigrants** came to the United States. They came for many reasons. Some came to find jobs. Others fled hardship and war. They hoped for better lives.

The Statue of Liberty and the New York coastline were welcome sights for newly arrived immigrants.

Many immigrants came to the United States by boat. They saw New York City in the distance. But they could not go there right away.

The boats landed at Ellis Island. The immigrants went to a big building with tall towers. They went through the **immigration** station.

Fun Fact

Many immigrants came through Ellis Island. Annie Moore was the first. She was 17 years old. She came from Ireland with her family in 1892.

 Immigrants entered the main building of Ellis Island when they arrived in the United States.

Ellis Island was an immigration station from 1892 to 1954. The island is in the Upper New York Bay. Immigrants had to stop there before entering the United States.

Chapter 2

History of Ellis Island

Ellis Island was a US military base for most of the 1800s. But in 1892, it became an immigration station. More than 400,000 immigrants came through Ellis Island that first year.

 People wait in line to go through the immigration station.

Immigrants went through an entry process. The first stop was the baggage area. Workers checked their bags.

The second stop was the Registry Room. It was a crowded open hall. Immigrants waited in lines. They went through **inspections**. Immigrants answered questions about their name, age, and home country. They also saw a doctor. Sick people could not enter the United States.

 Immigrants showed travel papers and answered questions from workers.

The busiest year was 1907. More than one million immigrants came to Ellis Island. But over time, immigration slowed. New laws made it harder for people to immigrate. Also, there was war in other parts of the world.

Ellis Island was a **holding center** during World War II (1939–1945). The US government forced people from Germany, Italy, and Japan to stay there. These nations were enemies of the United States.

The station finally closed in 1954. Immigrants entered the United States in other places.

Fun Fact

Immigrants traveled to Ellis Island from Italy, Ireland, and many other countries.

 The immigration station emptied after it closed in 1954.

But President Lyndon B. Johnson saw the importance of Ellis Island. He made it a **monument** in 1965. The buildings had not been used in 11 years. Workers **restored** the buildings. They also restored the Statue of Liberty.

The Statue of Liberty

The Statue of Liberty is located near Ellis Island. Immigrants could see it when they arrived. The statue shows a woman holding a torch. It is a symbol of freedom. The statue gave many people hope. They dreamed of starting new lives.

The statue was built in France. It was shipped to the United States. It came in pieces. Workers finished putting it together in 1886. The statue is a symbol of friendship between France and the United States.

The Statue of Liberty is made of copper.

Chapter 3

Immigrant Stories

Immigration is an important part of US history. Immigrants help shape US **culture**. They make the country **diverse**. But many people found the process of immigrating to be difficult.

Immigrants have helped make the United States the diverse country it is today.

The inspection at Ellis Island was hard for many immigrants. Some could not speak English. They relied on **interpreters** for help. Interpreters could speak more than one language. They helped immigrants communicate. Still, some immigrants were turned away.

Fun Fact

Some immigrants became workers at Ellis Island. They were good interpreters. They knew what the immigrants were going through.

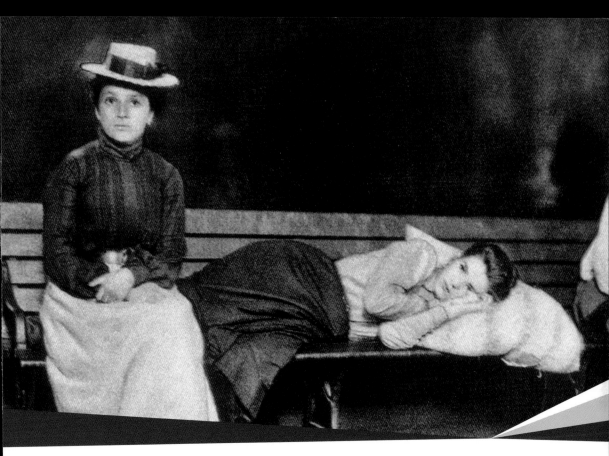

 Not all immigrants were allowed into the country. They had to wait for a boat back to their homeland.

Knud Larsen immigrated to the United States in 1923. He came from Denmark. He did not speak English. It was hard for him to understand people at work.

 Many immigrants lived with other immigrants in communities such as Little Italy in New York City.

Sometimes people laughed at him. He had to learn a new language. It was challenging.

Immigrants who made it through Ellis Island faced other hardships. Many had to find new ways to make money. They had to learn new skills.

Giuseppe D'Amico's family lived in New York. His parents came from Italy in 1903. D'Amico had a hard time finding a job. He knew how to be an electrician. But those jobs were not open. So his sister taught him how to sew. He became a dressmaker. He worked in a dress factory for many years.

Chapter 4

Visiting Ellis Island

Visitors can take a boat to Ellis Island. The island has two parts separated by water. The first part has a museum and a **memorial**. People can tour this section of the island.

 One part of Ellis Island is open to the general public.

Visitors can explore the Ellis Island Immigration Museum. This museum opened in 1990. It shows the history of the immigration station.

The museum is in the old station. It has three floors. The first floor has a gift shop and food. The second floor is the Registry Room.

Fun Fact

More than three million people visit Ellis Island every year.

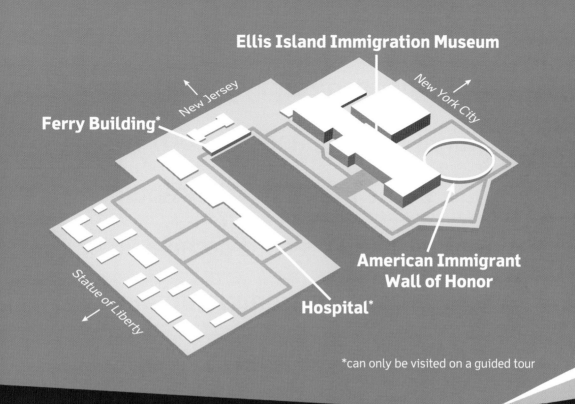

Ellis Island Immigration Museum

New Jersey

New York City

Ferry Building*

Statue of Liberty

American Immigrant
Wall of Honor

Hospital*

*can only be visited on a guided tour

It looks like the original room used by immigrants. The third floor has more displays. It also has a balcony that looks over the Registry Room. There is much for visitors to see and learn.

The American Family Immigration History Center opened in 2001. It is part of the museum. The center has a passenger record archive. It has records of the immigrants who came through Ellis Island. People can try to find their family's records.

Outside the museum is the American Immigrant Wall of

Fun Fact

Nearly 12 million immigrants came through Ellis Island over 64 years.

Immigrants who came through Ellis Island can find their names on the Wall of Honor.

Honor. It is a large, circular wall. It has the names of immigrants on it. This memorial remembers all immigrants to the United States. It honors their place in the country.

FOCUS ON
Ellis Island

Write your answers on a separate piece of paper.

1. Write a letter to a friend describing the immigration station at Ellis Island.

2. Why do you think immigrants had a hard time adjusting to life in the United States?

3. Which year was the busiest year for immigration at Ellis Island?
   - **A.** 1890
   - **B.** 1907
   - **C.** 1954

4. Why did many immigrants have to learn new skills?
   - **A.** They did not have skills before they came.
   - **B.** Certain jobs were not open to them.
   - **C.** Their parents made them learn new skills.

5. What does **communicate** mean in this book?

Interpreters could speak more than one language. They helped immigrants communicate.

    A. to make something known to others
    B. to listen carefully
    C. to write down answers to questions

6. What does **fled** mean in this book?

Others fled hardship and war. They hoped for better lives.

    A. moved closer to
    B. stayed in one place
    C. moved away from

Answer key on page 32.

Glossary

culture
The way a group of people lives; their customs, beliefs, and laws.

diverse
Having a lot of variety.

holding center
A place used to lock people up.

immigrants
People who move to a new country.

immigration
The process of moving to a new country to live permanently.

inspections
Careful checks to make sure something is acceptable.

interpreters
People who can speak two or more different languages and help people understand one another.

memorial
A structure built to remind people of a specific person or event.

monument
A building or structure that is of historical interest or importance.

restored
Returned something to its original condition.

To Learn More

BOOKS

Baker, Brynn. *Life in America: Comparing Immigrant Experiences.* North Mankato, MN: Capstone Press, 2016.

Carney, Elizabeth. *Ellis Island.* Washington, DC: National Geographic, 2016.

Kravitz, Danny. *In the Shadow of Lady Liberty: Immigrant Stories from Ellis Island.* North Mankato, MN: Capstone Press, 2016.

NOTE TO EDUCATORS

Visit **www.focusreaders.com** to find lesson plans, activities, links, and other resources related to this title.

Index

Answer Key: 1. Answers will vary; 2. Answers will vary; 3. B; 4. B; 5. A; 6. C